I HOPE YOU STAY

I HOPE YOU STAY

COURTNEY PEPPERNELL

Andrews McMeel
PUBLISHING®

ACKNOWLEDGMENTS

There are never enough words to express how grateful I am to be able to share poetry books with the world. It is because of a team of people that all of this is possible, and I could not do what I do without them. James, for your guidance and being the voice of reason in my mind. Lindsay, for your support and being the second pair of eyes I need. Briana, for your encouragement and organizing just about everything in this chaotic life we lead. And Ryan, for your illustrations that always bring my visions so perfectly to life.

Special thank-you to the care, direction, and creativity of Andrews McMeel Publishing—especially, Kirsty, Fred, Patty, Elizabeth, Holly, and Diane. Your dedication to every project I bring to the table is forever appreciated.

To my wife, Rhian, I couldn't complete any of these journeys without you. I love you with my whole heart. To my family—your unwavering support, encouragement, and belief in me through everything I set my mind to is something that truly drives me.

Finally, to my readers—I truly feel like I share a bond with you all, and it is this bond that I cherish with everything I have. Thank you for all your support, I can't wait to see what the future holds.

All my love,
Courtney

INSTAGRAM: @courtneypeppernell
TWITTER: @CourtPeppernell
WEBSITE: courtneypeppernell.net
EMAIL: courtney@pepperbooks.org

Before the light breaks and enters the dawn of a new day. You will have thoughts in your mind and feelings in your heart. You will have shadows of dreams that sometimes tear you apart. But the most important thing to remember is all the thoughts and feelings are yours. You may bend, but you will not break, and the light of a new day will ease all the ache. No matter the distance or what may come your way, from my heart to yours, I hope you stay.

IN YOUR HEART

You will ache   1

You will dream   43

You will love   85

You will heal   127

You will rise   171

YOU WILL ACHE

There was never a right time to say goodbye. Not
when you looked at me, with all that misery in your
eyes. But I couldn't keep up with all the lies, or
the way you treated my heart. I couldn't shake the
feeling, every time we kissed, like I was just another
name to add to your list.

I hold all this blame

    about how badly

    things between us ended

I dream so vividly

    of our conversations

    late at night

But despite all the reasons

    I shouldn't think of you

    I still do

It was just bad timing

I told myself

But bad timing happened

time and time again

And after all the pain

maybe it wasn't the timing

Maybe we were just two people

bad for each other

I used to picture us in rocking chairs, out on the porch. We'd be waiting for our grandchildren coming up the drive. But now that picture's gone, and every time I see those rocking chairs, yours is empty.

My heart lay asleep in a glass jar, kept safe on my shelf. Until you walked into my life and promised to be gentle, promised to help. So, I gave the jar to you, asked you to hold on tight, and instead you did the opposite. The jar shattered, and my heart fell to the floor. Now my heart is ripped and torn from all the pieces of glass, and I don't know what to do. All this mess, because I believed in you.

Everybody said to let you go, said we were no good together. So, I walked away, after too many fights in the back of the cab. But your memory stayed, and it follows me everywhere. I close my eyes and we're on the beach, sitting cross-legged, talking about all the places we want to go. I turn over in the sheets and the pillow still smells of your perfume. Tell me how I am supposed to move on when I'm haunted by all the things you are.

Did you mean to make my world stop turning? Do you remember the moment we stopped working? Why are you holding on when we are so clearly lost? If you ever even loved me, then break my heart quickly, because the ache is killing me slowly.

You are somewhere else, with someone new,
drowning in her scent, hands lost in her hair. And
yet I'm still here with all the moments we shared, not
knowing how I'm supposed to have those moments
with anyone else.

We sat in your car, with leftover takeout, and you listed all the things wrong with us. But all I could think about was how I wanted to fix what we'd broken. Thinking back now, even after all the time you've been gone and everything we've been through, what broke my heart that night was when you said, "You'll find someone new."

The grief lies in the space between us. It's made a home in the nights we don't speak and the days we ignore each other.

Will anyone

    love me

    the way I am

Will the loneliness

    in my heart

    be filled

Will the way

    I love

    ever be enough

She sat in the car the other night, the headlights shining over the driveway. She clicked the remote to open the electric gate, but it stopped, spinning on the gears, stuck in movement, unable to go further. And she felt her life as this, wanting to come home but stuck in the driveway, so close but so far away.

The universe stares back from her mirror

cloudy and unsure

And part of her wants to take a hammer to the glass

slip out of the world and into another

Somewhere she will be happier

All the messages left unopened

piled up in my phone

I knock three times

a secret code

but nobody's home

The rain falls

the sky full of sorrow

Your shirts still in my wardrobe

from all the times I borrowed

Scattered thoughts

from the things I could have done

The times I should have stayed

alone in this lonely tower

trying to forget

the future we could have made

Every playlist filled with sad songs

and poems about a girl I used to love,

and now I'm dancing all alone.

She will grieve a broken heart

But she will not break

We were meant to be together until the world ends.
But the world is still alive, spinning, carrying on. Yet
my world is crashing, stuck, holding on.

Somewhere in between the tears and the constant waiting, she forgot her worth. She forgot what it means to be the sun, the stars, and the sea. She forgot what it means to love and to live and to be happy.

All the people who have hurt you don't deserve to be in your life. They belong in the past, with all the ache. You need to move into the future and fill it with light.

She felt like the only house in the street, with lonely doors and lonely windows. All she wanted was for someone to light the fireplace.

People tell her she owes so many apologies to herself, to forgive all the mistakes she made. But maybe the stars need to forgive her too, for every night she looked away.

Even if you think the song is ruined because you shared it with them, it's still just a song. So many other people in the world have different memories with the same song. Lay all the ache you feel when you hear it to rest and create new memories.

She is scared to love again, because people change their minds. She is scared to love again, because people leave with no answers, and she is sick of thinking it's because of her.

So, she built a tiny garden and filled it with plants and spices in jars. And she told herself each day they grew, they would mend all the scars.

She gave her heart to someone who dropped it over and over again. Giving chances as though they were breaths. But now she is taking every chance back, and she will breathe clearly once more.

She is tired of the promises that seem empty. Of believing magic may fix her broken heart.

She has seen mountains grow from dust, and rivers forge, chasing their own paths. She has heard the call of the wind, reminding her to begin again.

She called the name a thousand times over, listening as it echoed. A name as hollow as a rugged canyon. Yet no answers returned, of why they left, of why the heartbreak flourished and the memories remained. But she must ache, and she must feel so that the sun will rise again.

I keep hoping for you. Hoping you will walk back
through the door. But the dishes are piled up
and the fridge is empty, and the rain comes every
midafternoon. I am closing my eyes more often than
not, hoping that the healing will come soon.

She is out there, somewhere in the wild, looking for herself.

You can lose, without ever really having.

By now, she is fluent in ache. How it spills into her veins and sits in her bones. If this ruin is all she has known, where will she find strength?

You can sew the scars, with stitches made from forgiveness. You can sprout new life, grow into your skin, and take back the fearlessness.

The world defines "disaster" in so many ways, but lately "disaster" is all my thoughts of you.

She likes the idea of new skin and hair regrowing, of new clothes and different memories and belongings. She likes that she can let go of the past and all the hurt and grow into someone new.

She built cities in her own mind, filled them with love and interest, and drove away the shadows. She hopes these cities will spill over into her world.

She began those first few months crying on her
bedroom floor. Boxes left unpacked, unsure of this
new life she was meant to lead. But then, one day, she
washed her sheets and showered in the morning; she
drew back the drapes and unpacked all her boxes.
She found a coffee shop down the road and cooked
dinner at home. She went on dates and bought fresh
roses. And even if there are still days of gloom, she
knows for every bad day, there is a good day, certain
to bloom.

A car horn sounds in the distance, and she steps away from the windowsill, the rain comes in steady, clouds had brewed all afternoon. The sky was as dark and unforgiving as she felt. But somewhere in between her tears, she saw the raindrops spelling out a silver horizon, and she knew all the pain would eventually disperse and the skies would brighten.

It is not always about the heart breaking. It's the uncertainty afterward. How unsure you become, about the way you look, how you dress, who you are. If they couldn't stay, then why would anyone else? But I am sure of you, sure you will grow again, grow new, grow more memories that you love and breathe through. You will be as beautiful as I believe you to be. Take your time, but do take the first step.

YOU WILL DREAM

That's when I realized the ache will always resurface.
Whether it's in the supermarket over a girl you
kissed who didn't kiss you back, or a boy who told
his friends about you but not his parents, or the job
you missed out on, or the sad movie you watched
alone on Friday night. The ache comes back around,
always in the moments your heart has room; but
maybe the ache has always wanted to be loved too.

She was taught to dream

    to imagine castles

    and sailing around the world

She was taught to live

    even though things are hard

    even though life can get you down

Here she was, comparing other dreams with hers, wondering if hers were big enough or bold enough or worthy enough to show off. But, darling, dreams are as big or small as you want them to be, the goal is to dream enough to be free.

Seek shelter in the arms of somebody who truly cares. Someone who pushes you to dream, who supports you, even in the moments hope is nowhere to be seen.

She is the kind of girl you spot sitting at the window of a café, with her nose buried in books, and her glasses at the tip of her nose. The kind of girl who hands you her change when you've left your wallet at home. She is the kind of girl who makes the smallest of moments seem like your greatest adventure.

You are home, and home can be many things. Right now, home is where I look, to cast away all the doubts I ever had.

On a windswept day, she sat at the beach. Sand whipping through her hair, salt from the sea finding her face. Her heart felt as heavy as the rocks facing the horizon. But she knew, beyond sea and sand, she would continue to carry her heart and hold her own hand.

I do not know of all your dreams, your hopes, your aspirations. But I know the feeling, to fall, to fly, and to fall again. Your wings never really break, sometimes they just need to rest.

Sometimes even in the silence, you can't hear
yourself think.

She is my soul, my heart, my life. The moment I
heard her laugh, I knew I wanted her to be my wife.

Pinpoint the moment you thought you could not go on, the moment you thought all your hopes would fall short, the moment you truly believed everything you worked for would desert you, take you back to the start. That moment often changes your course, but never your heart. Harness those feelings, and use it for greatness.

Each day, she opens her eyes and the light fills the world. Inside her, how she sees galaxies in coffee cups and wildflowers blooming in notebooks. She is a vision, a bird soaring high. She is the reason hope will fly.

What you dream of, the things you want to achieve, are as valid as you make them to be.

She was always in a faraway place; even in a crowded space, she was somewhere else. Thinking of other lives and how they may interconnect with hers. She dreamed of fields of flowers and running waterfalls, of sunlight falling over a face she would one day come home to. She planted feelings in potted plants and wore dresses the color of lilac. She loved harder than anyone I ever knew. She is the warmth of the fire when nights are cold. She is the person you want by your side, together as you grow old.

I hope when you fall, you have a soft landing, but even if you don't and it takes time for you to find your feet, know that you are worth every step.

She dreams of that voice, the one that calls to ask about her day. The way it sounds, even from far away, how it makes her sigh and her heart fill with color. That voice could never compare to another.

Fill your life with people who make you strive. Always thinking of the next day, always wanting to create, to challenge yourself. People who motivate you to keep going are important.

I think of you in the early hours of the morning, as the day is just beginning. I think of what we can be, together as one, as vast and as beautiful as the sky can be.

What I have come to know more than anything is that my soul grows and changes. There are moments it feels full, and others empty, but it continues forward, moving with every step I take in this life.

You will never be understood by everyone. Most people are still trying to understand themselves. The things you want to achieve are yours, and the people who try to push you into a corner aren't worth having in your life.

We always remember the ones who hurt us, who ruined our expectations or let us down. Perhaps, as we grow older, it's better to remember the ones who helped us. Even if they aren't around anymore, even if life got in the way or reasons out of our control meant we were just destined to spend a fraction of time together. We should remember how they made us feel, how they helped shaped us too, and we should carry that with us, in everything we do.

You still struggle some days with the idea of what you could have become versus what you are. But what you are is everything. What you are can be grown. Keep growing.

Don't use someone else to forget her. Don't shut
every door to keep from feeling. The feeling is what
keeps you moving, keeps you searching. Memory is
what makes us stronger, more determined. You need
to feel, all of it; you are never a burden.

It hurts to feel as though no one understands your secrets. As though you are the keeper of all these thoughts and nobody else could ever feel them too. But sometimes, on a rainy afternoon, you pick up a book and read it with some wine, and for the first time, someone understands. That even if the sun is shining, you don't feel the glow. But it's okay, because someone else in the world knows.

She saw her reflection in a snow globe, a different world inside. She's been afraid of changing, casting light upon shadows. But even tiny sparrows must leave home behind and seek the hills beyond.

Moments make us older, now I'm further away from who I was. I'm taking things slow, but I am still a child at heart, some things I barely know.

We're all happy and lonely, going and getting at the same time. We're chasing all the love and dreams we hope to find.

There are all these things you think you don't deserve. You wonder why all these roads are leading nowhere. But find me at the end of the tunnel, listen as my heart beats to the sound of your name. Listen as I promise, you deserve everything, especially to love again.

All the moments I feel like I'm drifting away from myself, I know your love and the way you make me feel is like nobody else.

You're the color

of my cure,

the light I adore.

You're the courage

I find in every day.

I would follow you

through the dark,

to any place,

with you

I want to stay.

In the times I felt most alone, I loved more than I have ever known.

You will feel lost for a while, like moments stopped in time. But it will be okay, you'll pick up the pieces and be just fine. I know it hurts, and instead of sleeping, you're dreaming of somewhere else. But the night is yours, please look after yourself.

Some of us sleep so soundly, with an arm around our waist, while others dread the night, lying awake thinking about someone we want so badly, it keeps us watching the clock.

But I wonder for all the nights

    I am

    wanting, needing, hoping

    for you

If I spent all these moments

    wanting, needing, hoping

    for all the things I deserve

    would I still be awake?

It is too heavy, the weight you carry all by yourself. How it troubles your heart. I wish I could carry it for you, I'd gladly take it so. But these are your boxes, filled of the things you struggle with. I know you are strong enough to build a castle and call it home; all I can do is remind you that you are not alone.

Are you really thinking about them, or just the idea of having someone?

I could lie and tell you that life will be easy, but I owe you more than this. Life is remembering to say please and thank you, watching sunsets when you need space to think, it's catching your breath after laughing until your sides ache, it's forgiving yourself when relationships break. It's returning the things you borrow and counting blessings, it's keeping promises and following your feet, it's dancing in the rain and pulling your hood up in the sleet. It's never expecting life to be fair, taking chances, being there when people need you. It's dreaming big and living small moments, it's holding hands in the cinema and drinking wine in a courtyard under fairy lights. It's remembering the things that make your heart swell and letting go of the things that keep you up at night.

My heart beats so loudly every time I see you behind the counter, it feels like a boom box playing every station full of love songs. I want to talk to you, not just to place my coffee order or tell you to have a nice day. I want to know your favorite color and if you enjoy the mountains, the theater, or ballet. I want to see you in the morning, not just for caffeine, I want to wake up next to you, kiss you, instead of all this daydreaming.

You achieve all your dreams by facing your fears. By experiencing the doubt and the disbelief and choosing to carry on anyway.

YOU WILL LOVE

That time of day when the light fades and the sky spills sleepy colors. That is where your dreams exist. If ever you need encouragement, to be reminded of why it's important to try, stop and look to the sky.

A long time ago, she used to believe all the roads in the world would not lead her to where she needed to go. But she's older now, and she knows roads crack in the heat and disappear in the snow, but if she places one foot in front of the other, eventually she will get to where she needs to go.

I don't tell you enough, this wonderful life you have given me. You have brought me years of laughter and umbrellas to my doorstep in the rain. You have brought home roses on difficult days and held me during nights of confusion and pain. You have shown me such kindness and adventures full of fun, but mostly you have shown me how to truly love someone.

Fall in love with someone who wants to learn
with you.

Some souls always find their way back to each other. It's a feeling you get, when you meet for the first time and you wonder if you've met them before. As though something deep inside you remembers the light in their eyes or the curve of their smile. The way they smell, the touch of their skin, the way they move down the corridor. It all feels so familiar, so strange. This is what the reunion of two souls feels like.

To this day

I have written books full of love notes

and yet my favorites will always be about you

The thing about you is that you never pulled away when I started to love you more. You are never impatient with my heart, I am never insecure with how you make me feel. I love you because you have never given me false hope.

It was the beginning of summer, just out with
friends, and I watched as you danced to your favorite
song. I don't remember the details of the night, but
I remember you and the way you danced. You were
so happy, so beautiful. I didn't believe in love at first
sight, until that night.

I never thought I'd be counting down the hours to see you again.

And whether she is the best thing to happen to you or the one who got away, you must let her live her own life.

We were in our favorite bar, already on the second glass of wine. And you leaned across the barstool, wrapped your leg around mine, pulled my shirt, kissed me for the first time. Now, I'd be lying if I didn't admit I'm always thinking about you and those red-wine lips. How you spun my world around, just with our first kiss.

I have always wanted a relationship that worked toward the future. I wanted to be able to picture Saturday nights curled up on the couch. I wanted to be able to think about decorating Christmas trees and finding art for the living room walls, I wanted to be able to see all the major moments in my life and having someone beside me for it all. This is what I believe deep, unapologetic love to be, when you can't imagine sharing all the beautiful moments without them.

We were in and out of hotel rooms, backpacking
through cities with skyscrapers and hiking
mountains at dawn. And I fell in love with the way
the sun touched your legs in the morning, how they
draped over mine. No photograph would be enough
to contain the memory I have of falling in love with
you over and over again.

Love story love

is really just the kind of love

when you find someone

who is compatible

with your own core values

I am more a hurricane than a gentle breeze some days. People bother me, annoy me with opinions that don't make sense and that don't add any balance to the world. I'm sick of everyone fighting, everyone waiting for their turn, instead of actual equality. I don't feel like being kind, I don't feel like being polite, I feel like screaming and cursing, moving the universe from sight. But then I am reminded of the littlest things in life, like the way bees make honey, and ants appear before rain, the way children say funny things, and how some musicians stay humble even after fame. I suppose even on the hurricane days, it's better to stay kind, for anger and bitterness really have no balance of mind.

You never need to give an apology

to someone who didn't want your heart

as much as your body

We grow old, and we always lose something. A lover, an old friend, a way of being. But shedding layers isn't always a bad thing. Remove what doesn't help you grow, instead let light and love in.

It's when your heart aligns with theirs. That's what love is. It won't matter how much you want a person, if their heart is somewhere else, lost, miles away, it won't work. Your heart cannot beat when another heart isn't on the same page.

It's hard not to fall in love with someone who looks at you one day and says, "Thank you for letting me be myself."

Some people need to lose someone before they understand that person's value. But I don't need that. I appreciate you, I need you, I couldn't imagine any day without you.

The way you strum that guitar, how those strings somehow make a melody. I wish I could write down all these feelings for you, but my heart feels too full. So, in case you were wondering, my heart has been yours for a long, long time.

How would I live this life without you? The way you make coffee on Saturdays, in the mug you bought, simply because it reminded you of me.

We were up for hours that night, sitting cross-legged on the living room floor, the lights off, the TV glare filling the space. You had boxes full of old DVDs, showing me which movies made you cry and which ones made you laugh. Which ones you turned off and which ones caused a flutter in your heart. And even if I was tired, eyes drowsy from too much wine, I could have listened to you for hours more, because the way you talk about the things you love is why it's you I adore.

Darling, I saw you standing there
and all the words fell away
Darling, you laugh and my heart
beats faster than I can say
Now, we're listening to records
in our own meant-to-be
Darling, forever you will be the
most important thing to me

Date who you want to date, love who you want to love.

Tongue tied and heart beating fast is how to live.

Some people get so mad seeing other people in love. And I don't know if it's jealousy or just wanting to stir things around. But watching people in love is not just inspiring, it's profound.

I've traveled the world, seen sunsets and mountains and city skylines. And my idea of love has been constantly changing, but if it means anything, I like the way love feels, when I look at you and it's like I have the whole world right beside me.

I love you,

like I love soup

on a cold winter's day.

How it warms me,

makes me feel at ease.

You hung hope around my neck, told me to wear it every day. You said the nights wouldn't be so lonely anymore. And I must admit, in the beginning I bet against us, thinking you would leave, and yet you proved me wrong. How happy I am you chose to stay.

I love to document our love. Each photograph makes the moments with you stand still, so I can hold them forever. Friday night and kissing you in the mirror; Sunday morning asleep in the sheets, sun draped over your bare back. Tuesday night drinking wine by the river; and midweek afternoons sipping coffee until the sky dims. We are building an album of moments, and in each one you are more beautiful than ever.

Be romantic. Arrange dinner plans at her favorite restaurant, bring her coffee in bed, write her a love letter, hold her hand during a late-night movie. Give without wanting in return; love is about giving more than gaining.

I don't know how you make my heart beat so fast
when you kiss me, or when you place your hands
on either side of my face, how my cheeks flush, hot
beneath your touch. But I know that every kiss I've
had before yours has never made me feel so alive.

One day, you will find a home, and it won't be a place, it will be a person. And you will be loved in spite of all the baggage and boxes you bring with you.

She wants a love so powerful it wipes out everything else.

But love means different things to different people.
It can be unexplainable, happen in mysterious ways.
Even if her whole life the moon has been told to only
love the night, sometimes instead she loves the way
the sun lights up the days.

Kiss to inhale the scent of someone you have dreamt of kissing. Kiss until you are dizzy, unable to remember any moments before this one. Kiss like it's the greatest thing you've ever done.

Write in journals the things you are grateful for, make time for an old friend, walk in the mornings as the sun is rising, spend less time focusing on your faults, spend even less time reading rants on social media, plant flowers, check the mailbox, cook a new recipe, dance in your living room. Be in love with living.

I love the way you make me feel. Like I am more than an afterthought, or a second guess, or a maybe. You make me feel like I am your first thought, only choice, a certainty.

Of course, there are different kinds of love. There is infatuation and physical and emotional love. There's respect and comfort love. There's the kind of love you ignore, the kind you can't stop thinking about, the kind you make work, the kind that seems impossible. But the love of your life embodies all love. That kind of love is all-consuming, emotional, physical, comforting. It doesn't matter how many times you say "I love you," at the end of the day, you know they will stay. True love doesn't run away.

You can say anything you want

But showing is different

You keep her by showing how much you love her

YOU WILL HEAL

She came home one night, peeled off all her clothes, wrapped herself in her robe. And she had been telling me about her day. Since the moment she walked through our bedroom door, absently playing with her hair, petting the dog, words racing and rolling over each other as she explained all the things that had happened. And it didn't matter to me if the next eighty years were spent listening to her day from start to finish, because I want to listen. I love to listen to her. This is how I know she is the one, because I can't imagine listening to anyone else.

Love can be found across oceans, or in coffee shops over long, drawn out days. It can be right around the corner or weekends spent boarding planes. Where love is found, there is life, even if life begins when we least expect it to.

The sunlight drifted through the window, in warm rays of yellow. The day whispering, *It's time to start again, I'm here for you.*

The tree bends, breaks, and lives through the storm, but despite the wind and rain, the roots still hold on to the earth.

You will split open, more than once in your life. You will feel raw, numb, all your thoughts laid out in front of you, pictures of your torn-up soul. But you will come home again, back to the parts that make you whole.

She will move on, tired of your mistakes and false promises. She will not reply to your "I miss you" texts, she will not answer your calls. Because while you were busy in the sheets of someone else, she was healing, finding strength, realizing that she was better off without you.

It may not always be clear, but the universe does want good things for you.

She loved to watch the storms roll in. The kind that cast shadows over the sky, thunder so loud you could hear it for miles. She would curl up beside the windowsill, a book in one hand, a mug of tea in the other, and she would enjoy the rain. The pounding raindrops, almost as loud as her heart, washing away the pain.

I hope you find time for yourself, in between the motions of the week and all the things that keep you up at night. In between it all, I hope you find a moment to breathe.

You are in control of your own progress, the only person who can decide how much or how little you tread. No one else gets to decide for you, no one else gets to tell you what defines your "getting better." All the things you struggle with are yours, your battles are yours, and your victories are yours.

On a cloudy day, I went to lunch with some friends. A
hidden maze of cafés wedged between old red brick
walls, and flower pots lining the stalls. I sketched
fingertips across white-tipped leaves, had coffee
near sunflowers, and breathed in fresh air. Then the
clouds parted, and the sun shone, and in that fraction
of a moment, the world felt healed.

All these sounds that take up living spaces, echoing
of first dates, a song of someone in love, a child
laughing at her father making faces, a friend holding
open the door, a traveler returning to familiar places.
All sounds of being alive, of wanting all this healing
to be so much more.

You will often ask yourself

    who was I back then

    who am I now

    who will I be

And even if you don't have the answer

I suppose the real journey

    is just to keep going

The space in your heart that opens and closes to love, how it will suffer, but oh how it will renew. Keep your pulse beating to all the love inside of you.

If you weren't here, the world would beat just a little bit differently. The stars might not shine the same, and the forest wouldn't whisper your name. The world needs you.

You need to be lost, to be on uneven ground. So, you learn, and you grow. When you struggle, you understand what being grateful really means.

Everybody heals in different ways, at a different pace. You are allowed to want to be wrapped up in someone else's arms, to fall apart and still hold your dignity. It's okay to want someone to rub your back and tell you everything is going to be fine. We fight the good fight, and we stand tall on our own, but sometimes it's just nice to be reminded you aren't alone.

What are you looking for

> Listen to others and yourself. When you listen
> to the way you act from others, you often find
> yourself becoming more self-aware. When
> you listen to yourself, you learn how to set
> boundaries for other people.

What do you want to be

> Do you like loud parties or small, intimate
> dinners; do you think about choices and
> consequences; are you there for others or only
> yourself? The hardest critic is yourself, but
> self-reflection is good for the soul.

What do I do when I fail

> You get back up. You will fail at many things
> in your life, sometimes over and over again.
> But the point is to continue forward; no matter
> how big or small the failure, you are always
> learning, always renewing.

It gets a little too much sometimes, on the nights I don't feel enough, hoping you won't walk away, that you'll always stay. But I'll never let go of the person I can be, because I'm so grateful you're here for me.

You've got to stop wondering if he's still thinking about you, a year after it came crashing down. You've got to stop holding on to the girl who was never right for you. Stumbling home in the dark, hoping you'll stop falling apart. But you are more than the tears that stain your pillows, more than the things out of your control. You are a fresh brew of tea, a sun-filled day in the middle of winter, a stitch to mend a break, life is not over just because you make mistakes.

She wants so much to feel alive, to pull back the covers. But it holds her down, anchors her to the shadows. And I know, I know, I know. I see all the grace inside you, how you shine.

Sometimes feelings are unstable, and people don't mean what they say. Sometimes words just aren't enough, and you lose your way. But we're still moving even if we feel still. Time keeps going, the universe keeps existing, and so should you.

She was shedding skin, out in the light of the moon. She knows when things don't feel quite right, she knows when it's time to focus back on the things that make her feel alive.

Share your story, but only when you are ready.

Just be honest, I am working on myself because I need to. There is no shame in prioritizing the things you need. Anyone who can't accept this isn't good for you anyway.

She knows love isn't always taking photos kissing on kitchen countertops, or roses when she's feeling down. It's arguing over things that seem unnecessary but eventually coming back around. It's healing after every disagreement and knowing you'll make the long road together.

I feel like I am sinking back into the soil, while everyone continues to grow, sprouting new buds and blooming, long before I can feel my roots.

Even if they aren't the best habits, they can still be broken. Create better habits for yourself, ones that remind you to feel alive.

Balance is giving to others and being grateful when others give to you.

It's how you see yourself and the expectations you
set. When you expect too much from yourself, you
begin to doubt the things you can do. When you
base your idea of perfection around ideas that aren't
achievable, you begin to believe you are not worthy.
But if you stop expecting so much of yourself and set
small, achievable goals, you begin to find courage,
even on the darkest days.

There were moments after we ended things, I
thought you would come back through the door. But
late one night, lying awake staring at the ceiling, I
realized all my energy, I would give no more. I am
better now, the scars still show, but I am healing
instead of feeling so low. I've grown patient with my
feelings, learned to let go, years from now I'll be so
happy, and you won't even know.

Self-care is messy. It is sometimes easy and other times difficult. But it's about continuation. Continue to look after yourself.

And sometimes

it's watching the same episode

over and over again

because it makes her feel better

I am not going to be or act a certain way for anyone. I am who I am, and I am going to embrace it. Not everyone will like me, but the most important thing is that I love me, all my parts, working together, all that makes me whole.

She has told you before how hurt she has been. How she has felt fragile and vulnerable with no one to pick up the pieces. She has told you that she cannot survive in between being loved or not loved enough. She has told you that she is all or nothing. So, if you respect her, you will not use her heart.

Struggle is with us all. Every day, a different story, a different path. So, when you feel you cannot go on, look around you, chances are there are others who feel they cannot go on too.

If they make you feel like your body, your heart, and your soul are not worthy of love, then they are not worthy to be loved by you.

There will come a day when they will no longer be your first thought in the morning or keep you up at night. But while they are, you mustn't be so hard on yourself or rush to heal the wounds. Our hearts live on with scars that run deep. Scars are never neat, but you don't have to force them to close if you are not ready.

What is the use in looking happy when inside you are hurting. People may tell you to hide, pretend, and fake it until you make it. But when you are as happy on the outside as much as you are on the inside, then you've really made it.

Healing and self-care are not only about the things you surround yourself with but also the people. Find people who are forgiving and patient and fair. Find people who show you kindness and accept you on the days you struggle. Find people who don't make you feel guilty for focusing on yourself.

So, you slept a handful of hours and managed half
a meal; so you walked to your front door, opened it,
and closed it again. You slept more hours than the
week before, you ate half instead of nothing, and you
got up instead of staying. That's stepping, just keep
stepping.

For every long moment a breath catches in the back of your throat, too weary to exhale, know that all your healing exists in the small details. At a party on a Saturday night, in the corner talking to a girl you just met, spilling your soul to a stranger because sometimes it's easier to talk to a new friend than an old memory you regret. A weekend drive on a long highway with the sun shining, and you're smiling because sometimes fresh air is better than not finding the words to say all you've been feeling and thinking. Turning a song up loud, because it makes you dizzy remembering all the things about yourself. You should be forgiving and not apologizing for living.

YOU WILL RISE

She will rise

     against wind and rain

and she will triumph

     despite the pain

She is real and honest with all the things she feels,
and this does not make her weak, this makes her
stronger than ever.

We all have walls, some higher than others, to fortify our hearts from the recklessness of selfish people. But we must let the light in, to soak deep into our skin, and rise each morning with purpose.

Take photos, put on lipstick, wear the dress you've been meaning to drag out of the closet. Embrace your goals, breathe deep through your mistakes. Be a boss.

You don't need to be anyone else

All that you are

is brighter than any star

I no longer want to be someone who tiptoes around people as though eggshells surround them. I want to overcome all the doubt and be the kind of person I would have looked up to when I was younger.

You don't need people in your life who

diminish your worth

make you insecure

question if you belong on Earth

I just want to hold her, kiss her, tell her that she's mine. I just want to taste her, touch her, tell her everything is going to be fine. How beautiful it is to love someone forever; how beautiful it is to be in love with a dreamer.

She unfolds herself in front of others, bares all her scars to show she is still here. She survived, and she wants you to know her story. She wants you to know the resilience is inside you too.

She was a little girl once with a dream, and through determination, hard work, and endless persistence, she became a woman with a vision.

We have risen, from closets and chains and lost love. We still have miles and miles to go, but one day, I hope saying "I'm in love" will be the only thing that really matters.

Sensitivity is such an honorable thing. Kindness is not weakness as much as there is power in forgiving. When you strip someone of emotions, they become just a shell; it is far more beautiful to let your emotions run wild.

You need to pause sometimes, to relish in the stillness and accept just sitting, removing all thought. Breathing through the troubles and hitting the renew button. It's so important to restore rather than destroy.

You don't need to drink to feel confident

You don't need to do drugs to dream

You can be high on yourself

Everyone says she's beautiful, but that doesn't mean you aren't. What is beautiful to someone isn't to someone else. And when you look at yourself and wonder whether you are beautiful, know there will always be someone who thinks you are. Try to let your beauty show, try to embrace yourself, try to remember you really do glow.

There are women who gently whisper, *You have lipstick on your teeth,* or smooth over a hair out of place. There are women who check that your dress looks perfect from behind and never let you leave the bathroom stall with toilet paper on your heel. These are women here for other women. We should be here for each other.

Words will not stop her, only drive her. She has a fire in her heart and determination in her step. People may tell her she is bound by gender, sexuality, and skin, but she knows better than to let hate win.

She has been many women, lost, fearless, exhausted, and brave. But above anything she is the kind of woman who will make you remember her name.

You do not love her if you expect her to not have her own opinion. You do not love her if you expect her to never have a say. You do not love her if you expect things to always go your way. You love her when you hold her heart and she holds yours, and together you walk through every door.

She is more than perfume and tinted eyes. More than pretty clothes and stretch marks. She is more than golden hair and turning heads to stare. She can move mountains, take empires with her mind. She will rise to every opportunity and take every setback in her stride.

I know that I love you, because you help me to
believe I am capable of anything. You make me feel
as though I can hold the weight of the sky, even in the
moments I get a little shy. I have battled dark days,
sometimes questioning my warmth, but with you I
feel as though all this power has been unearthed.

All these people walking around putting emphasis on what you look like, dress like, and whether you're beautiful because they say so. But isn't it about your soul, and how you treat your waiter, and the way you let your kindness grow.

Things happen because of your involvement and your drive to make it happen. Things happen because you put your heart and soul into achieving all your goals. Rising from ashes is so much sweeter when you know you've worked for clear skies.

One day someone is the best thing to ever happen to you, and the next they are the worst. But even if you feel like good days are not coming and the heartbreak will last forever, know that it will pass. You will meet someone new, and eventually the love will last.

To the person I was never meant to be with, thank you for showing me what I didn't need. Thank you for making me realize I didn't have to settle, that I could be with someone who wanted the same things I did. I know that I am worthy of love and kindness and someone who loves me equally. Thank you for showing me that.

Remind your daughter, your mother, your
grandmother, your aunt, your sister, your cousin,
your friends that you are stronger together. That the
world needs balance, that womanhood is a blessing.

You don't need to feel guilty for feeling so much. For wanting to be more than a flame—a firestorm. You are the center of the house, the glue that holds it all together, the light that keeps it warm.

When you are told not to speak, you realize the power in your voice. You must stay strong in your values, your wants, your compassion. Fight for your freedom, as there is no other choice.

She knows what it is like to feel betrayed, abandoned, left out in the cold. But it's because of this loss, she feels the undeniable pull to always be honest, fearless, and bold.

How many of us have seen strength in a woman
wielding a sword, leading battlefields, mapping plans
for victory—know that sometimes battle is also in the
quieter moments, like standing up for what is yours,
speaking encouragement to the women around
us, supporting each other when life gets us down,
helping her up when she feels she might drown.

The world is full of people who will make you feel as though your success is not warranted, but you must ignore these people. You rose from soil and dust, and you fly so high, you deserve every bit of sunshine.

We are our own person. We have hopes, we struggle, we dip in and out of the roller coaster that is life. But we are stronger than we sometimes believe, and it is this strength we must look to in times of trouble.

Why are we taught to criticize, to compete, to judge?
We compare bodies, minds, abilities. We should
teach each other instead to embrace, love, and
encourage our capabilities.

In the end, we all become memories to someone. So, you should fill yourself with love and light and be a memory someone will cherish.

You are more than the lines on your body, your shape, your skin. You are the start of day, when life begins.

Your passions are the things that make you who you are. The spark in your eye when you speak of your passions should be what someone loves most about you. Never let anyone tell you that your hopes and dreams don't matter.

She felt alone, inside her mind, as though she was
no longer at home. So, I brought blankets for when
she was cold, reminded her to eat, left flowers by
her bed. Despite knowing the light was hers to
find, I wanted to remind her that her heart deserved
another who was kind.

Unleash yourself to the world, shout from rooftops
that you are worthy to rise. Turn back anyone who
fills your space with negativity and lies.

As you grow, you will do so with a little more wisdom, a path lighted with healing, a mind daring for answers. And you will continue moving forward, onward and upward to better things.

We must stand up for each other.

In difference, there is learning, and in humanity, there is understanding.